Novels for Students, Volume 16

Project Editor: David Galens

Editorial: Anne Marie Hacht, Sara Constantakis, Ira Mark Milne, Pam Revitzer, Kathy Sauer, Timothy J. Sisler, Jennifer Smith, Daniel Toronto, Carol Ullmann **Research**: Sarah Genik

Permissions: Debra Freitas, Shalice Shah-Caldwell
Manufacturing: Stacy Melson

Imaging and Multimedia: Lezlie Light, Kelly A. Quin, Luke Rademacher **Product Design**: Pamela A. E. Galbreath, Michael Logusz © 2002 by Gale. Gale is an imprint of The Gale group, Inc., a division of Cengage Learning Inc.

Gale and Design® and Cengage Learning™ are trademarks used herein under license.

For more information, contact
The Gale Group, Inc.
27500 Drake Rd.

Farmington Hills, MI 48331-3535
Or you can visit our Internet site at http://www.gale.com **ALL RIGHTS RESERVED**
No part of this work covered by the copyright hereon may be reproduced or used in any form or by any means—graphic, electronic, or mechanical, including photocopying, recording, taping, Web distribution, or information storage retrieval systems—without the written permission of the publisher.

For permission to use material from this product, submit your request via Web at http://www.gale-edit.com/permissions, or you may download our Permissions Request form and submit your request by fax or mail to: *Permissions Department*
The Gale Group, Inc.
27500 Drake Rd.
Farmington Hills, MI 48331-3535
Permissions Hotline:
248-699-8006 or 800-877-4253, ext. 8006

Since this page cannot legibly accommodate all copyright notices, the acknowledgments constitute an extension of the copyright notice.

While every effort has been made to ensure the reliability of the information presented in this publication, The Gale Group, Inc. does not guarantee the accuracy of the data contained herein. The Gale Group, Inc. accepts no payment for listing; and inclusion in the publication of any organization, agency, institution, publication, service, or individual does not imply endorsement of the editors or publisher. Errors brought to the attention of the publisher and verified to the satisfaction of the publisher will be corrected in future editions.

ISBN 0-7876-4899-X
ISSN 1094-3552

Printed in the United States of America
10 9 8 7 6 5 4 3 2 1

That Was Then, This Is Now

S. E. Hinton 1971

Introduction

Susan Eloise Hinton, known to her multitudes of readers as "S. E. Hinton," a trick that she and her early publisher used to mask her gender, is credited with revolutionizing the young adult book industry with the 1967 publication of her coming-of-age book, *The Outsiders*, which she published when she was only seventeen years old. Her second effort, 1971's *That Was Then, This Is Now*, also dealt with the realistic themes of youth violence and tragedy that had characterized her first work, and some critics considered this sophomore effort even better than the first. Both books, and in fact most of Hinton's books, are based on events that she witnessed as a teenager in Tulsa, Oklahoma. *That Was Then, This Is Now* tells the tale of Bryon Douglas, a six-teen-year-old greaser who finds himself growing up and growing apart from his foster brother, Mark, whom he adores. As Mark refuses to accept responsibility for his actions and gets involved with selling drugs, Bryon must face the hardest decision of his life—whether to turn Mark in. With its graphic depictions of gang life, the hippie lifestyle, and the potentially crippling effects of drugs, *That Was Then, This Is Now* offered a snapshot of the turbulent and transitional times in which it was written and has stood the test of time, becoming a favorite with teens, adults, and educators.

Author Biography

Susan Eloise Hinton, known to her readers as S. E. Hinton, was born in Tulsa, Oklahoma, in 1950, a setting that has influenced the majority of her young adult novels. In fact, Hinton is commonly credited as the person who revolutionized the tone of young adult fiction, by using gritty, realistic settings such as the Tulsa-like background of her hugely successful debut novel, The Outsider. Published in 1967, when Hinton was seventeen and a student at Tulsa's Will Rogers High School, the book also set the standard for future young adult novels, by addressing hard issues that teens faced, such as gang violence. The novel was published under her initials, because the publisher feared that their audience, mainly young men, would not accept a female author, especially since most of her narrators are male. Even though Hinton's gender was eventually revealed, she has used her initials for all of her published books thus far.

Hinton's second young adult novel, *That Was Then, This Is Now*, featured the same type of setting and themes that made *The Outsiders* such a success. However, since *That Was Then, This Is Now* was published four years later, in 1971, it also addressed current issues, such as drug use, and examined the hippie lifestyle. Both *The Outsiders* and *That Was Then, This Is Now* were made into film adaptations, and the former was directed by *Godfather* director, Francis Ford Coppola. Hinton was actively involved with both adaptations, which featured such future stars as Emilio Estevez, Matt Dillon, Patrick Swayze, Rob Lowe, and Tom Cruise. Two other Hinton novels, *Rumble Fish*, published in 1975, and *Tex*, published in 1979, were also adapted as films. Coppola also directed *Rumble Fish*, which he filmed in black and white to emphasize one character's color blindness. Hinton's most recent works include two children's books, *Big David, Little David* and *The Puppy Sister*, both published in 1995. Hinton continues to live and work in Tulsa, Oklahoma.

Plot Summary

Chapter One

That Was Then, This Is Now begins when the narrator, Bryon Douglas, and his foster brother, Mark, both teenagers, go to one of their favorite hangouts, Charlie's Bar, a rough pool hall where they often try to hustle people for money. Later, they find their hippie friend, a kid with the nickname M&M, who tells them that his sister, Cathy, is home from private school. They hang out for a while, but M&M gets bored and leaves. Mark and Bryon follow, just in time to stop some gang members from beating up M&M. Mark, Bryon, and M&M start walking home, and Mark suggests they beat up somebody else. M&M yells at them for their hypocrisy, and Bryon reflects on what M&M has said.

Chapter Two

The next day, Mark and Bryon go to the hospital to see Bryon's mother, who has just had an operation and who says they should visit a beaten-up kid across the hall. Bryon goes downstairs to the hospital's snack bar, where he meets Cathy, M&M's sister who is back in town, and asks her out. Bryon talks with the severely beaten-up boy, Mike Chambers, who tells Bryon that he got beaten up after he saved a young black woman from being harassed by his own gang members. Mike drove the woman home, and when he dropped her off, she told her friends to kill him. Mike tells Bryon that he does not hold it against the woman, and Bryon sees some merit in his point of view, although Mark does not.

Chapter Three

Bryon looks for a job but does not have any luck, even with Charlie, who tells him that he needs to change his ways before anybody will hire him. Charlie lets Bryon borrow his car, however, and Bryon asks Cathy to the school dance. At the dance, Bryon and Cathy are the center of attention, since nobody recognizes her. Mark gets knocked unconscious with a bottle, after he tries to stop somebody from attacking Ponyboy Curtis, one of his friends. Bryon realizes that his ex-girlfriend, Angela Shepard, set up the attack on Curtis and vows to get revenge on Angela.

Chapter Four

The next morning, Bryon returns Charlie's car and finds out that Charlie has received his draft notice to fight in Vietnam. Bryon and Mark reminisce about their gang childhood together and how life has changed since then. Bryon simply says, "that was then, this is now." At school the next day, Bryon is very reflective and feels separate from everybody else. The next week, the school principal catches Mark driving his car. The principal does not press charges because Mark explains that he needed to borrow the car so that he could get to his weekly parole appointments, which, ironically, are for Mark's past history of stealing cars. Bryon notes that Mark can get away with anything.

Chapter Five

Bryon and Mark go hustling one night, and Charlie tells them that the army is not going to draft him, because of his police record. Bryon and Mark hustle two rough Texans, who ambush them after the bar closes, holding them at gunpoint in the alley. Charlie comes to their rescue but gets killed in the process. The police give Charlie's car to Mark and Bryon. Unlike Mark, Bryon feels guilty about Charlie's death and begins to spend more time with Cathy, who understands him.

Chapter Six

The Texans are caught, and Mark and Bryon testify at the trial. Bryon's mom is in the hospital for a month, and Bryon decides to take Charlie's advice and clean up his appearance and his attitude so that he can get a job and help pay bills. Cathy tells Bryon she thinks M&M is doing drugs. One night, Bryon, Mark, Cathy, and M&M go cruising down the Ribbon—a popular, two-mile-long strip of restaurants, drive-ins, and supermarkets—and M&M takes off with some friends, saying he's never coming back.

Chapter Seven

M&M does not come home the next day, and Bryon and Cathy spend every night for a week driving down the Ribbon looking for him. Bryon gets a job at a supermarket and starts to bring in some money. Mark also brings in money, which Bryon assumes is from gambling. Bryon and Mark go out cruising together one night and pick up Angela. Mark gets her drunk until she passes out and then cuts her long hair off, getting back at her for setting up the fight at the dance. At home, a drunk Bryon cries about all of the bad stuff that happens to people, and he wishes M&M were okay. Mark says he knows where he is, and he will take Bryon there.

Chapter Eight

The next day after work, Mark directs Bryon to a house in a rundown part of town. The people in the house know Mark and call him "Cat." Mark asks about "Baby Freak," M&M's hippie name, but he's not there. Bryon goes to Terry Jones's place that night for a party. While he's waiting on the porch for the others to show up, Angela's brothers and two other guys attack him, beating him badly for cutting Angela's hair. When Bryon wakes up, Mark is there. Bryon asks him not to get even with the Shepards, saying he's sick of all of the getting even and wants to drop it.

Chapter Nine

On the way home from the hospital the next morning, Mark is frustrated that Bryon will not let him get even with the Shepards. Cathy comes to visit Bryon at home, and Bryon tells her he loves her and says he has a lead on where M&M might be staying. That week, Bryon makes a visit to Charlie's grave, thanking him for saving his life. Two nights later, Bryon and Cathy go to the hippie house, where they find M&M huddled in the corner of a room, crashing from a massive LSD-induced hallucination. Cathy calls her father, who meets them at the hospital.

Chapter Ten

The doctor tells them that M&M will never be the same, although Bryon tries to reassure her that M&M will get better. At home, Bryan is lost in thought, reflecting about how much his life has changed. Desperate for a cigarette, he looks in Mark's secret stash, where he finds a canister of drugs. In a flash of insight, he connects Mark's selling drugs with M&M's condition and calls the police to turn Mark in. Mark comes home and tries to defend his actions, but Bryon realizes clearly, for the first time, that Mark has no sense of right or wrong. The police take Mark away, while he keeps asking Bryon why he's doing this.

Chapter Eleven

Bryon wakes up the next morning, unsure that he was justified in turning in Mark. Bryon finds he no longer loves Cathy and pushes her away. He testifies against Mark, whose blatant, unrepentant confession gets him five years in the state reformatory. Bryon devotes himself to work, where he gets promoted from sack boy to clerk. At the end of the summer, Bryon visits Mark, who looks hardened and dangerous from his brief time in the reformatory. Bryon tries to apologize, but Mark tells him he hates him and never wants to see him again. When Bryon refers to their past good times, Mark throws Bryon's words back at him, saying, "that was then, this is now." Mark is sent to the state prison; Bryon notes that he has lost the ability to care. He constantly replays the last year's events in his head, trying to figure out if things could have turned out differently. He is unsure of anything and mourns his lost youth, wishing that he could go back to simpler times, when he used to have all of the answers.

Characters

Baby Freak
See M&M

Bryon's Mother
See Mrs. Douglas

Cathy Carlson

Cathy Carlson is Bryon's girlfriend; it is out of his love for her and concern for her brother M&M that Bryon decides to turn Mark in for dealing drugs. Cathy is a shy, innocent teenager, who comes back from private school when she runs out of money. Unlike Bryon's exgirlfriend, Angela, Cathy does not get jealous and is a good influence on Bryon. This influence puts her at odds with Mark, who feels he and Bryon are starting to grow apart. This becomes more noticeable after Charlie dies saving Bryon and Mark and Cathy understands Bryon's feelings of guilt, whereas Mark does not. Cathy worries that her brother, M&M, whom she loves very much, is smoking marijuana and, since he is so trusting, may end up taking LSD as well. She says that M&M is not happy because he gets so much harassment at home over his hair, and so M&M has started hanging around other places.

Cathy is distraught when M&M runs away, and she and Bryon drive up and down the Ribbon every night for a week, looking for her brother.

After Bryon gets beaten up by the Shepards, Cathy comes to see him at home, where he lets her know he has got a lead on M&M's whereabouts. When Bryon gets better, Cathy goes with him to the hippie house where M&M has been staying. She is horrified when she sees the effects the LSD has had on her brother but still finds the strength to call her father and drive M&M to the hospital. Cathy is distraught when the doctor tells them that M&M may never be the same but is comforted by the love and affection that Bryon shows to her throughout this ordeal. This makes it all the more difficult for Cathy the next day, when she goes to see Bryon, after hearing that Bryon turned Mark in to the police for dealing drugs. Bryon is no longer in love with her, and she can tell. They never speak again, and she starts dating Ponyboy Curtis, although M&M says that she liked Bryon the most.

Mr. Jim Carlson

Jim Carlson is Cathy's dad, whose constant criticisms of his son, M&M, help to drive M&M out of the house and into using drugs. Bryon first meets Mr. Carlson when he picks up Cathy for their date, and he can see how he antagonizes M&M over the length of his hair and because he is flunking math and gym. When M&M leaves home, Mr. Carlson thinks that it is a phase and that he will be back, but as Cathy projects, he does not. Mr. Carlson likes Bryon, especially after Bryon helps find M&M and gets him to the hospital. Mr. Carlson is a wreck when he sees the effects that the drugs have had on his son and is concerned that the news will devastate his wife.

M&M Carlson

M&M Carlson, Cathy's thirteen-year-old brother and one of Bryon's friends, has a bad experience with LSD, which motivates Bryon to turn in Mark for dealing drugs. Even M&M's family call him by this nickname, which he earned for his addiction to the candy of the same name. M&M is the consummate hippie. He wears his hair long, wears an old, loose-fitting army jacket everywhere he goes, and has a metal peace symbol on a rawhide cord around his neck. He is extremely trusting, and even tough characters like Charlie think he is nice, if a little weird. He is thankful that Bryon and Mark save him from getting thoroughly beaten by Curly Shepard but is frustrated at Mark's hypocritical suggestion that they beat somebody else up that same night. M&M tips off Bryon that his sister is home, which helps Bryon figure out who Cathy is when he first meets her.

M&M is not happy at home, mainly because his father constantly criticizes him about his long hair and his bad grades in math and gym. As a result, he starts hanging around more often with other hippies, who introduce him to marijuana.

After M&M gets fed up at home and runs away, he moves into a hippie house, where he earns the name "Baby Freak," since he is several years younger than everybody else in the house. It is here that he experiments with LSD, a much more potent drug. When Bryon first goes to the house with Mark, M&M is not there, but somebody else says that he is "flying" and that he is going to "crash." Later, when Bryon takes Cathy to the house, they find him huddled in the corner of a room, in the after-math of a massive LSD-induced hallucination, in which spiders have been eating him and colors have been talking to him. When Bryon runs into M&M at the end of the story, he tells Bryon the long-term effects of his LSD trip—he may have flashbacks, he might not be able to have normal children, and his grades are not good anymore, since he cannot remember much. Also, M&M does not want kids, which is different from before his acid trip, when he used to say he wanted a large family. M&M also tells Bryon that Cathy is dating Ponyboy Curtis but that he knows that Cathy liked Bryon the best. This news, however, does not affect the emotionally detached Bryon.

Mrs. Carlson

Mrs. Carlson is Cathy's mother, who worries that her husband is giving their son, M&M, too much grief about his long hair. When M&M is at the hospital getting treated for his LSD hallucinations, her husband worries how she will take the news.

Cat

See Mark

Mike Chambers

Mike Chambers is the beaten-up teenager in the hospital, whose story and viewpoint help to inspire Bryon not to hate others and to stop the endless cycle of violence. Mike belongs to a gang from a different neighborhood, and one night some of his gang members start picking on a young black woman. Mike sticks up for her and then gives her a ride home, but she still tells her friends to kill Mike, and they beat him very badly. Mike tells Bryon and Mark that he does not hold it against the woman.

Charlie

Charlie is a twenty-two-year-old bar owner, who dies while saving Bryon and Mark from two Texans whom they have hustled. Charlie is the older brother of one of Bryon's exgirlfriends, and he sometimes gives Bryon and Mark Cokes on credit at his bar. His tough reputation ensures that Bryon and Mark always pay him back. It is this same reputation that has earned him respect from both the police and Charlie's tough customers. Charlie tries to warn Bryon and Mark that they should be careful whom they hustle, but they do not listen. Charlie receives his draft notice for the army, to go fight in Vietnam, but in the end, they do not take him because he has a police record. He gets this joyous news shortly before he dies. The police are impressed with Charlie's heroic act in saving Bryon and Mark and give the two boys Charlie's car. Later in the story, Bryon takes a trip to Charlie's grave, where he thanks his dead friend for saving his life and letting him use his car.

Media Adaptations

- *That Was Then, This Is Now* was adapted as a film in 1985, directed by Christopher Cain, written by Emilio Estevez, and starring Craig Sheffer as Bryon, Estevez as Mark, Kim Delaney as Cathy, and Morgan Freeman as Charlie. Hinton assisted with the production of the film, which is available on video from Paramount Home Video.

Ponyboy Curtis

Ponyboy Curtis is one of Mark's friends, although Bryon holds a grudge against him because Curtis had the good sense to stay away from Angela Shepard. Actually, as Bryon learns, Curtis, a quiet and shy teenager, had no idea that Angela was interested in him, although he does know that Bryon is mad at him for something. At the school dance, Mark introduces Curtis to Cathy, and Bryon is wary, although he soon realizes that Cathy is not interested in leaving him for Curtis, as Angela did. Bryon finds new respect for Curtis at the dance, after he lets Bryon know that Mark has been hurt. Although Cathy makes jokes to Bryon about Curtis asking her out—when she wants Bryon to—at the end of the story, Curtis and Cathy do start dating, when Bryon pushes her away.

Dirty Dave

The man who calls himself Dirty Dave is one of two Texans who attempt to beat up Bryon and Mark after they hustle him and his friend at pool. Both Texans are sentenced to life in prison after they kill Charlie, for which Bryon and Mark testify against them.

Bryon Douglas

Bryon Douglas is the narrator of the story, in which he tells how he and his foster brother, Mark, grew apart and how he made the decision to turn

Mark in for dealing drugs. When they are kids, Bryon and Mark are inseparable troublemakers and love each other like brothers. When they are sixteen, however, they start to grow apart, as Bryon begins to become his own person, while Mark wants to cling to their mutual past. Still, Bryon and Mark care about each other. For his part, Bryon shows it by taking care of Mark after he gets cracked on the head with a bottle in a fight and by taking a beating for Mark by falsely claiming the blame for cutting off the hair of Bryon's ex-girlfriend, Angela. Bryon undergoes a major transformation in the story, which begins when he and Mark talk to Mike Chambers and Mike's story of getting beaten up and not wanting revenge resonates with Bryon. Bryon's feelings of moral responsibility increase when he feels guilty over the fact that Charlie lost his life while saving them. Bryon's emotional journey includes falling in love with Cathy, who is the first girl he actually cares about.

When Bryon's mother ends up in the hospital for a month, he decides to clean up his act and get a job. When M&M runs away from home, Bryon helps Cathy find him and helps her take him to the hospital after he has a bad LSD hallucination. When he finds the drugs that Mark has been selling and connects them with M&M's condition, he decides once and for all that Mark does not know right from wrong and turns him in to the police. Although he is not sure he made the right choice, Bryon testifies against Mark. From this point on, Bryon becomes emotionally detached and pushes Cathy away. He does not see Mark again until a few months later, when he tries to apologize. However, Mark tells him he hates him and never wants to see him again. At the end of the story, not even the news that Mark has been sent to prison affects Bryon, who has lost the ability to care. He constantly replays the last year in his head, trying to figure out what would have happened if he had done something differently. He yearns for his youth, when he had all the answers.

Mrs. Douglas

Bryon's mother, Mrs. Douglas, is known for her tendency to try to help stray animals and people, as she does when she adopts Mark after his parents kill each other. Bryon's mother is in the hospital for much of the story, for reasons that are never made known, other than she has had surgery. She encourages Bryon and Mark to talk to Mike Chambers, a boy in the hospital who was beaten by several black men after he tried to help a young black woman. She lets Bryon and Mark live their own lives, trusting that when they stay out late or get into trouble, they are smart enough not to get caught. When Mark starts bringing in a lot of money from his drug sales, she starts to wonder where it is coming from but, like Bryon, does not ask Mark. After Bryon has turned Mark in, she tells Bryon that she does not hate him and that he should not hate himself. She is also optimistic that Mark will learn his lesson and come home, whereas Bryon knows that is not possible.

Terry Jones

Terry Jones is one of Mark and Bryon's friends, who factors into the major beatings of both Mark and Bryon. When Mark and Terry are at the school dance, Terry provides the beer bottle that Curtis's attacker later uses on Mark's head. Likewise, when Bryon gets beaten up by the Shepards, it is while he is waiting at Terry's house for everybody to show up for Terry's party.

Mark

Mark is Bryon's foster brother, whom Bryon turns over to the police when he finds Mark dealing drugs. Mark, whose last name is never mentioned, comes to live with Bryon and his mother after Mark's parents kill each other in a drunken fight over the illegitimacy of Mark's birth. When they are kids, Mark and Bryon hang around in the same gang, break the same laws, and love each other like brothers in the process, which is still apparent at sixteen. Mark gets Bryon a new shirt for Bryon's first date with Cathy, refuses to leave Bryon's side when the two Texans they have hustled ambush them, and takes care of Bryon after Bryon is beaten by the Shepards. However, while Mark desperately tries to cling to the gang personality, Bryon begins to embrace his own adult identity, and the divide between them grows. Whereas Bryon feels guilty over the fact that Charlie lost his life while saving them, Mark does not show any remorse, one of the examples that makes Bryon realize Mark has no concept of right and wrong.

Mark does not understand when Bryon begins hanging out with Cathy instead of causing trouble with him, and he dislikes Cathy as a result. Mark is also frustrated when Bryon will not let him continue the cycle of violence by getting even with the Shepards, especially since it was Mark who cut off Angela's hair. When money is tight, Bryon goes out and gets a job at a supermarket, but Mark's police record prevents him from doing the same. Since he wants to help bring money into the household, too, Mark starts selling drugs to hippies, who call him "Cat." He does not feel that this is wrong, since he does not take any himself and since he does not push it on people. Because Mark is active in the drug world, he knows where M&M is staying and shows Bryon. When Mark hears Mike Chambers's story, he says he would never be able to forgive somebody who hurt him that badly, a promise he makes good on after Bryon gets him put away for drug dealing, and he tells Bryon he never wants to see him again. In the end, Mark refuses to clean up his act and gets sent to the state prison.

Second Texan

After Bryon and Mark hustle him at pool, the unnamed Texan holds the boys at gunpoint in an alley, while his friend, Dirty Dave, prepares to beat them with brass knuckles. Both Texans are sentenced to life in prison after they kill Charlie, for which Bryon and Mark testify against them.

Angela Shepard

Angela Shepard is Bryon's exgirlfriend, who broke up with him in favor of Ponyboy Curtis, although she tried to win him back when Curtis did not realize she existed. Angela is stunningly beautiful, but Bryon notes that it is wasted beauty, since Angela has a tough-as-nails personality and is not very nice. At the school dance, Angela gets one of her friends to attack Curtis, but Mark steps in, getting cracked in the head with a bottle. When Bryon realizes that Angela set up the fight, he vows to get even with her. Shortly after Bryon and Mark are ambushed by the two Texans, Angela gets married to one of her brother's friends, thinking she is pregnant with this man's child.

Later that year, after M&M disappears, Bryon and Mark run into Angela on the Ribbon. She is extremely drunk and goes for a ride with Mark and Bryon when Mark says he will get her more alcohol. For one of the first times in her life, Angela breaks down and cries on Bryon's shoulder, telling him she is miserable in her marriage and that he is the only one for her. When Angela passes out, Mark cuts off all of her prized long hair. The next morning, Angela tells her brothers, Tim and Curly, that Bryon did it, prompting them to beat Bryon up, even though Angela saves her pride in public by telling everybody else that she had decided to cut it off. At the end of the story, after Bryon has turned in Mark, Angela runs into him and tells Bryon that it was a low thing to do.

Curly Shepard

Curly Shepard is one of the older brothers of Angela Shepard, Bryon's exgirlfriend. He helps beat up Bryon after Mark cuts off Angela's hair. Curly belongs to the Shepard Gang, led by his older brother, Tim. While Bryon considers Tim a real hood, he thinks Curly just plays the part, even though he has spent time in prison.

Tim Shepard

Tim Shepard is one of the older brothers of Angela Shepard, Bryon's exgirlfriend. He helps beat up Bryon after Mark cuts off Angela's hair.

Themes

Coming of Age

That Was Then, This Is Now is the story of Bryon Douglas's coming of age during his adolescence. When the story starts, Bryon is concerned only about himself and Mark. Early in the story, however, he meets Cathy, M&M's sister, and falls in love with her. As they begin dating more, Bryon notes, "I had quit thinking only about myself." And when M&M runs away and Bryon comforts a crying Cathy, he realizes that "it was the first time I'd ever felt bad for anyone except Mark." Bryon also makes the transition from feeling that he can do whatever he wants to and get away with it to somebody who makes sacrifices and who understands that his actions have consequences. For example, in the beginning of the story, Bryon notes that he really needed a job, but that nobody would hire him. Charlie gives him a tip, saying that he should really look inside himself and he would see "the reason why you haven't gotten a job before now." Later, after Charlie is dead and Bryon is starting to change his views, he realizes what Charlie was talking about and asks himself, "Who's going to hire a mouthy kid who acts like he already knows it all?" Bryon sucks up his pride and gets a "haircut, clean clothes, and a really big change in attitude." Unfortunately, Bryon is aware of his transformation, and also is aware that "I was changing and [Mark] wasn't."

Violence

Bryon's and Mark's lives are saturated with violence, and they jump at the chance to save M&M from getting beaten up by Curly Shepard and his gang: "Me and Mark looked at each other, and Mark flashed me a grin. We both liked fights." M&M, however, does not like fights and criticizes Bryon and Mark when Mark notices a black guy and suggests they "jump him." Says M&M, "You just rescued me from some guys who were going to beat me up because I'm different from them, and now you're going to beat up someone because he's different from you." Although M&M's words have little effect on Mark, Bryon starts to think about what he's said and realizes that in the past he has not liked it when he "was the one getting mugged."

Bryon's uncertainty towards violence as a solution increases when he talks to Mike Chambers, a young gang member who got beaten up by a young black woman's friends after he tried to help her. Although most gang members Mike's age would find a way to get even, Mike does not hold it against the woman. Bryon can see Mike's point "about not hating the people who beat him up," but Mark does not.

Topics for Further Study

- The Vietnam War influenced the lives of many young American men who were called upon to fight in a war in which many did not believe. Research the political and social climate in America during this time period and write a journal entry from the point of view of a young man who has just been drafted.

- Hinton was a teenager when she published her first young adult novel, which she hoped would resonate with other teens who had similar experiences. Write a onepage synopsis for a young adult novel based on observations you have made about your high school or other teenage experiences.

- Although the majority of reviewers credit Hinton with creating realistic tales, some maintain that teen life in the 1960s, even in gangs, was not as bad as the author's depictions. Research gangs and gang life during the 1960s and discuss how the actual history of the time period compares to Hinton's depictions.

- In the story, the narrator, Bryon, turns in his foster brother to the police and, as a result, loses the ability to care about anyone. Study current psychological research that addresses instances in which people experience loss of emotions. Using your research to support your claims, give a diagnosis of what you think happened to Bryon.

- Study the current methods that the government and public service organizations are using to fight drug distribution and use. How have these methods been effective? How have they failed? Propose your own idea for how to fight the war on drugs.

Although they have been accustomed to violence since they were kids, it takes on a darker tone when Mark gets in a fight and gets cracked "across the side of the head" with a beer bottle and has to be taken in an ambulance to the hospital to get stitched up. When Mark realizes that Angela set up the fight, he finds an opportunity later to get her drunk and cut off her hair. Because Angela's brothers think Bryon has done it, they continue the cycle of violence and beat Bryon badly. He ends up with a "black eye ... stitches in my lip," and "smashed ribs." After Bryon gets beaten, Mark wants to "go look up the Shepards," but Bryon stops him. "I don't want to keep this up, this gettingeven jazz ... so if you're planning any get-even mugging, forget it." Bryon thinks back to Mike Chambers and realizes that, just as Mike did not hate his attackers, "I didn't hate the Shepards either."

Gang Life

While Bryon comes of age and embraces his adult identity, Mark desperately tries to cling to the gang life that they enjoyed as kids. Says Mark, "It was great, we were a bunch of people makin" up one big person, like we totaled up to somethin" when we were together," and that "it's kinda sad, really, when you get to where you don't need a gang." Although Bryon tries to get Mark to see that it is good "when you know your own personality so you don't need the one the gang makes for you," Mark is unsure and still yearns for the past, when "we were like brothers, not just you and me, but all of us together. We woulda died for each other then." Although the gang is not as close as they used to be, the violence inherent in their surroundings still prompts occasional displays of support. For example, when somebody tries to attack Ponyboy Curtis with a bottle, Mark puts himself at risk by stepping in between them, saying, "Hey, come on, man, fight fair," for which he earns a crack on the head with the bottle. And as mentioned above, when Bryon gets beaten up by the Shepards, Mark immediately wants to go and get even with them. This idea of protecting one's gang members extends to friends who are not technically part of the gang. When Bryon and Mark are about to be beaten by the two Texans whom they have just hustled, Charlie saves them, threatening the men with "a sawed-off shotgun." Even when the men shoot at Bryon, Mark, and him, Charlie "slammed both of us to the ground," a heroic act that saves Bryon and Mark and kills Charlie in the process.

Responsibility

Along with Bryon's other transformations in his emotional journey, he comes in touch with his sense of moral responsibility. When he was younger, Bryon "wasn't above taking a pack of cigarettes from a drugstore, but that was about it." Bryon is willing to steal small things but cuts himself off at a certain point. Furthermore, as he notes, "I still felt that stealing was wrong." Mark, on the other hand, "was really bad about stealing things" when he was a "kid." And, as Bryon notes, "Mark couldn't see anything wrong with stealing stuff." When Charlie dies trying to save Bryon and Mark, after he has already warned them about hustling, Bryon's seed of moral responsibility blossoms, and he feels really bad for the first time in his life. "I couldn't get it out of my mind, Charlie's warning us about hustling." As he tells Mark, "Charlie is dead! He was all set for life, he wasn't gonna get drafted, he had his business ... and then we blew it for him." Mark, however, refuses to believe they are responsible, saying, "he knew those cowboys had a gun, he knew what kind of a chance he was taking."

At the end of the story, when Bryon finds the drugs Mark has been selling, he realizes that 'Mark had absolutely no concept of what was right and what was wrong; he didn't obey any laws, because he couldn't see that there were any." Bryon thinks about Cathy, M&M, and the pain her family is going through, and he feels that it is his responsibility to turn Mark in: "M&M was in the hospital, and maybe he was messed up for life—and Mark was selling the stuff that made him that way."

Alcohol and Drugs

Like violence, the community that Bryon and Mark live in is rife with alcohol and drugs, both of which are shown to lead to bad consequences. Mark's attacker uses one of the beer bottles from the "six sixpacks" that Terry Jones sneaks into the school dance, to hurt Mark. Likewise, Mark uses alcohol to make Angela pass out so that he can cut off her hair. M&M's marijuana smoking leads him to try stronger "stuff" like LSD, which has many longterm effects, including the possibility of having "messed up" kids. This is devastating to M&M, who originally wanted "a large family."

Style

Narration

The story is told in the first person viewpoint, from the perspective of Bryon Douglas, which is consistent with Hinton's other teenage novels. By doing this, Hinton imbues her book with a deep sense of emotion. In the beginning, Bryon notes that "Mark was my best buddy and I loved him like a brother." In the end, Bryon is emotionally dead and says, "I don't even care about Mark. The guy who was my best friend doesn't exist any longer, and I don't want to think about the person who has taken his place." Along the way, Bryon leads the reader through all of the ill-fated steps that led to this transformation. Had Hinton used a third-person narrator to tell Bryon's story instead of letting Bryon tell it, the feeling for the character would not be as personal, and the shocking ending, where Bryon turns Mark in for dealing drugs, would not have as much impact.

Foreshadowing

While the ending has impact, the careful reader can pick up on a number of Bryon's statements that foreshadow Mark's drug dealing and his resulting feelings for Bryon when he is put away. The first of these happens after Bryon and Mark visit Mike Chambers in the hospital. Although Bryon sees how

Mike could forgive his attackers, Mark says that he could never forgive anybody who hurt him that badly. In an offhand comment to the reader, Bryon responds to Mark's comment by saying that, at the time, he did not think much of Mark's statement, "later I would—I still do. I think about it and think about it until I think I'm going to go crazy." Although most readers have not been given enough information to realize that Bryon is talking about Mark's eventual hatred for him, readers are still left to wonder what happens in the future to make Bryon think so hard about this statement.

Mark's eventual career as a drug dealer is also foreshadowed. Later, when Bryon is trying to get a job, Mark tells him, "I'm goin' to start bringin' in some money," and "I ain't gonna sponge forever." Mark does not say how he is going to bring in money, but to Bryon, that is not as odd as why Mark said it. Up until this point, Bryon notes, Mark had "never said anything about being dependent on us." Still, Bryon does not question him on it. Neither Bryon nor his mother question Mark when he starts "bringing in money … more than he ever had before." Bryon tells the reader that at the time he had assumed that Mark was winning the money by playing poker, but Bryon also goes on at length about the issue in this passage, which signals the reader that the reality was different from what Bryon had thought at the time. Bryon draws attention to Mark's income again later on, saying that Mark was "spending more and more time away from home" and that even Bryon's mom, who normally does not pry into Mark or Bryon's business, is "bugged about where he was getting the money." Although Bryon "still figured he was doing some serious poker playing," the way that Bryon sets this up leads the reader to believe that it is something more than that, a setup that pays off when Bryon finds the drugs and realizes "Mark was a pusher. That was where he was getting his money."

Irony

Irony is the unique awareness that is produced when someone says something and means another, or when somebody does something, and the result is opposite of what was expected. In *That Was Then, This Is Now*, the irony is the latter: situational irony. In this case, Hinton employs the irony for tragic purposes. Out of his love for Cathy and concern for M&M, Bryon sacrifices Mark by turning him into the authorities. However, in a cruelly ironic twist, this act causes him to lose his love for Cathy: when she stops by the next day, he is cold to her, knowing that he is "hurting her," but not caring. Bryon notices the change in himself even as he is saying the hurtful things, and he wonders "impersonally why I didn't love her any more. But it didn't seem to matter." He also realizes that to him, M&M is "just some brother of hers in the hospital … not my friend, not somebody I too cared about." In fact, Bryon realizes, "I don't seem to care about anything any more. It's like I am worn out with caring about people." Although Bryon makes this realization calmly, it is devastating for the reader, who can still care and who feels the effects of Hinton's tragically ironic tale.

Historical Context

Vietnam and the Antiwar Movement

The 1960s and early 1970s were turbulent times, and the war in Vietnam did not help abate this tension. The conflict in Vietnam had actually begun in 1946, shortly after World War II ended. WWII had left many areas in Southeast Asia unstable, and over the next two decades, the United States quietly provided support to South Vietnam and those allied with the country, which was fighting against Ho Chi Minh's Communist forces in North Vietnam. The United States, so fearful of the spread of Communism that it viewed the loss of Vietnam as the start of a "domino" effect in Southeast Asia, escalated its involvement in the area. In 1964, President Johnson asked Congress for support, after one United States destroyer—performing a covert operation—was attacked by North Vietnamese forces off the coast of North Vietnam and another was allegedly attacked. (Later, it was shown that the second destroyer had not been attacked.) Johnson, who assured Congress that the destroyers were on routine, overt missions, convinced Congress to pass the Tonkin Gulf Resolution, which effectively gave Johnson unlimited power to escalate the Vietnam conflict. At this point, most Americans were unaware of these happenings.

By 1965, when fifty thousand new United States ground troops were added to the twenty-three thousand already stationed in Vietnam—posing as military "advisors"—the American public was more educated—much to the government's dismay. As James S. Olsen and Randy Roberts noted in their 1996 book, *Where the Domino Fell: America and Vietnam, 1945–1995*, "The decision to Americanize and militarize the conflict in Vietnam jump-started the antiwar movement in the United States." Olsen and Roberts note that in 1965 alone, "more than thirty other antiwar organizations sprouted," joining the existing groups. Much of the resentment came from the numbers of American troops required to feed the war machine. As J. M. Roberts notes in his *Twentieth Century: The History of the World, 1901 to 2000*, "In 1968 there were over half a million American servicemen in Vietnam."

Compare & Contrast

- **1960s–1970s:** The United States significantly escalates its military involvement in Vietnam, prompting the government to "draft" its young men to fight and igniting the antiwar movement. Many young Americans enroll in college—the only legal way to avoid being drafted—stage protests, burn their draft cards, and even flee to other countries to avoid having to fight in the war.

Today: After an unexpected attack on the Pentagon in Washington and the World Trade Center in New York City, the United States engages in a full-scale, international war on terrorism. The American public rallies to support this decision, and the military experiences a surge in its ranks as patriotic young men and women enlist to help wage the war.

- **1960s–1970s:** Many hippies and other members of the counterculture movement—who are often in their twenties or younger—experiment with "recreational" drugs to expand their minds and rebel against the establishment. For some people, these drug experiments backfire and cause permanent brain damage or other side effects that limit the person's ability to function in society.

  Today: America's public service organizations help to fight the war on drugs through influential advertisements that depict drugs as a barrier to success. These ads are aimed mainly at young children and teenagers, the primary target of many drug pushers.

- **1960s–1970s:** The peace symbol,

tie-dyed shirts, and other wild developments in fashion become symbols for hippies, who use their unconventional clothes as one of many ways to express their desire to rebel against the establishment.

Today: Many teens who want to appear trendy wear "retro" clothes and jewelry from the 1960s and 1970s, although they do not necessarily follow the hippie way of life. In addition, these clothes are often produced by large corporations, which are part of the establishment that the hippies were rebelling against.

In order to meet these numbers, the United States government relied on the Selective Service System to "draft" young American men into the war. In *That Was Then, This Is Now*, Bryon notes the affect that draft notices had on many Americans, when he returns Charlie's car to him after the dance and tries to talk to him: "He didn't seem too interested, but he was having his own troubles. He'd got his draft notice." Although Charlie is ultimately saved from being drafted because of his police record, many others were not and showed their protest against the war by burning their draft notices, staging public demonstrations, or fleeing the country, usually to Canada. By the time the United States government admitted defeat and began to withdraw its forces in 1973, the war had claimed the lives of fifty-eight thousand American men.

Hippies and Drugs

During the war, as the casualties rose, those involved in the antiwar, counterculture movement reacted in different ways, some violent, some not. One of the most enduring images from the era is that of the "hippie," derived from the word, "hip," meaning somebody who is trendy. Unlike some of the more militant antiwar groups, hippies believed in freedom, peace, and love, a philosophy that was often expressed through nature imagery such as the flower. In fact, a famous example of this "flower power," as David Steigerwald cited in his *The Sixties and the End of Modern America*, was during the hippies' march on the Pentagon in 1967: "Protesters sang to the troops, called for them to 'join us!,' and stuck flowers in gun barrels." However, while Steigerwald notes that hippies staged their protests using these and other nonviolent methods, such as creating a line of people by "locking arms and sitting down," he also notes that their opponents did not always reciprocate. The same Pentagon demonstration is a good example: "The marshalls ... made a serious assault, dragging protesters out of their lines and beating them with billy clubs." In *That Was Then, This Is Now*, Bryon, a "greaser" who loves to pick fights, notes his own reaction when he and Mark jump their first hippie: "I hadn't realized those guys refuse to fight back, and what happened to the one we got hold of, it made me sick ... after that we left them alone."

In addition to their nonviolent demeanor, hippies, like M&M in the story, were also characterized by their long hair and deliberately shabby clothes, in an attempt to embrace their freedom and rebel against the establishment. One of the other major ways in which hippies achieved these goals was through the use of recreational drugs. As Terry H. Anderson noted in his *The Movement and the Sixties*, "freaks," another name for hippies, commonly used dope—marijuana and hallucinogens like LSD—to "expand sensory perception and 'blow the mind.'" However, as Anderson notes, experienced hippies stayed away from drugs that led to a "bad trip." In Hinton's story, M&M earns the nickname "Baby Freak" because he is so much younger than the other hippies. Also, when M&M takes some LSD, the pusher who gives it to him tells Bryon and Cathy that he is "on a bad trip." Like M&M, whose brain is permanently damaged from the LSD, historian Martin Gilbert noted that the "'drug culture,'" which gained influence in the early 1960s, poisoned "the minds of millions of people."

The Civil Rights Movement and Racial Tension

In the 1960s, the Civil Rights movement was in full swing. Civil rights leaders like the Reverend

Martin Luther King, Jr. and Malcolm X inspired African Americans to protest the discrimination and segregation they had experienced in the United States. In some cases, as with the hippies, blacks staged peaceful demonstrations. However, in the late 1960s, amid growing tensions between whites and blacks, racially motivated riots broke out in major cities such as Los Angeles, New York, Chicago, and Detroit.

Critical Overview

That Was Then, This Is Now belongs to a class of books known as young adult novels. However, in 1971 when the book was published, this field was completely different. In fact, Hinton herself helped to inaugurate the new tone of the field with her immensely successful young adult novel *The Outsiders* (1967), which was published when Hinton was a teenager herself. As she noted in *Speaking for Ourselves*, the lack of books for young adults in the 1960s was disconcerting: "If you were through with the horse books and not ready for adult books there wasn't much to read except *Mary Jane Goes to the Prom*, and I couldn't stand to read that stuff." Hinton thought that other teenagers, like herself, might want to read about books that dealt with real issues.

This was especially true, since some teenagers had for years been reading controversial adult books like *Catcher in the Rye* (1951), a fact that in turn helped to invoke the ire of self-imposed censors. Unfortunately, Hinton's tendency to discuss realistic themes in her young adult novels has also landed books like *That Was Then, This Is Now*—with its overt violence and drug references—on censored book lists.

Fortunately, the book has fared better in the reviews. Published four years after *The Outsiders*, *That Was Then, This Is Now* was a relief for Hinton, who had suffered from a huge case of writer's block since she had published her first novel. As Jay Daly noted in *Presenting S. E. Hinton*, "the cycle was broken at last upon the insistence of her boyfriend (and husband-to-be), David Inhofe," who was a student with her at the University of Tulsa. Reviewers were delighted at the new book, having waited eagerly for another Hinton book for five years. An overwhelming majority of reviewers noted the similarities to the *The Outsiders*, such as Michael Cart of *New York Times Book Review*, who called both books "powerful, realistic stories about being young and poor." Others remarked on the graphic themes of the book, such as Sheryl B. Andrews, who called it "a disturbing book" that "will speak directly to a large number of teenagers" and that "does have a place in the understanding of today's cultural problems." On a similar note, *Times Literary Supplement* called the book both "violent and tender," "a punch from the shoulder which leaves the reader considerably shaken."

However, not everybody adored the book, and as Hinton has published more books, some critics have gotten more vocal. In his 1986 essay, "Tough Puppies," *The Nation's* Michael Malone criticized the idea many popular and critical reviewers have that Hinton's books are realistic. Citing the unrealistically brutal violence and neglect, Malone said that "it is difficult, if not horrifying, to think that millions of 12-year-olds ... find any more in them than the most remote connections." Malone concluded that "despite their modern, colloquial tone," Hinton's novels are "fairy tale adventures."

The next year, Daly also questioned the validity of early criticism, but for different reasons. Daly considered *That Was Then, This Is Now* "more disciplined" and "well-crafted" than *The Outsiders* but said that it "was not necessarily better." However, as Daly noted, he believed that many other critics had the "tendency to enshrine *That Was Then, This Is Now* without looking too deeply," which Daly surmised was "a belated climbing-on-the-band-wagon of *The Outsiders*." Daly also thought some reviewers, like Andrews, mentioned above, "seemed to dislike the book but could not quite bring herself to say why," so instead she retreated "to the safe haven of the sociologist-critic position."

In the end, the attempts to ban Hinton's books or the questionable criticism about *That Was Then, This Is Now* have not made much difference. Hinton and her books—whose timeless themes resonate with people from different generations—have continued to find success with popular audiences.

What Do I Read Next?

- Eve Bunting's *Someone Is Hiding on Alcatraz Island* (1984) features the story of Danny, a San Francisco boy who saves an old woman from a mugger's attack. Unfortunately, in the process, Danny offends the Outlaws, a gang at his high school. He tries to escape to Alcatraz Island, but the gang follows, and Danny, with the help of a park ranger, must survive on the grounds of the old prison. The book was published in reprint edition in 1994 by Berkley Publishing Group.

- *The Chocolate War* had a very controversial reception when it was first published in 1974. Robert Cormier's popular and groundbreaking novel features the story of Jerry Renault, a freshman at a Catholic high school, who does the unthinkable when he inspires a movement in refusing to sell chocolates for the school fundraiser, even though his actions eventually provoke the retaliation of the Vigils, the school gang. The book was published in a reprint edition in 1986 by Random House.

- Hinton's *The Outsiders* (1967), the

unexpected smash success that paved the way for grittier young adult novels, including *That Was Then, This Is Now*, details the struggle between two gangs, the poor greasers and the rich Socs (short for socials). In Hinton's book, the greasers were the ones who normally got attacked by the Socs, which flipped the standard model of violence on its head. The book was published in a reprint edition by Prentice Hall in 1997.

- Hinton's *The Puppy Sister* (1995) is technically a children's book, but, like her young adult novels, Hinton's book has been enjoyed by people of all ages. The story is pure fantasy and features the tale of a young puppy who does not realize that she is a dog. She decides that she can become a human, and, through sheer will she does, a transformation that involves the whole family. The book was published in a reprint edition by Bantam Books in 1997.

- Hinton's third novel, *Rumble Fish* (1972), continues to explore the life of street teens, in this case, Rusty-James, who fights with his fists and has always been bailed out by his older brother when his own fists were not enough. Rusty-James's life is torn apart through a cataclysmic series of events, and for once his brother is not around to save him. The book was published in a reprint edition by Laurel Leaf in 1989.

- Hinton's *Taming the Star Runner* (1988) deviated from her normal style by using a thirdperson narrator to tell the story of troubled fifteen-year-old Travis Harris, who is sent to his uncle's Oklahoma ranch as an alternative to juvenile hall. Although Harris is reluctant to adapt to his rural surroundings at first, he eventually develops a relationship with Casey Kincaid, a horse trainer —who is in the process of training the stallion, the Star Runner—and publishes a book about his life. The book was published in a reprint edition by Laurel Leaf in 1989.

- Hinton's books often concern the story of gangs or gang members in young America, particularly in the 1960s and 1970s. *Gangs in America III*, edited by C. Ronald Huff and published by Sage Publications in 2001, is a popular anthology that collects the most up-to-date information about contemporary gangs and the current law enforcement efforts used to prevent and control gang violence and crime. Through a series of essays, the contributors thoroughly examine how and why young people join gangs, the effects gangs have on communities, and the newest potential solutions.

- Paul Zindel's *The Pigman* (1968) tells the story of John and Lorraine, high school students who pass the time by playing phone pranks on people. Through one of these pranks, they meet "The Pigman," a sad widower named Mr. Pignati, who changes their lives forever and gets them to see that their actions have consequences. The book was published in a reprint edition by Bantam Starfire in 1983.

Sources

Anderson, Terry H., "Hippies and Drugs," in *The 1960s*, edited by William Dudley, Greenhaven Press, Inc., 2000, pp. 200-01, originally published in *The Movement and the Sixties*, Oxford University Press, 1995, pp. 259-60.

Andrews, Sheryl B., Review of *That Was Then, This Is Now*, in *Horn Book Magazine*, Vol. XLVII, No. 4, August 1971, pp. 388-89.

Cart, Michael, Review of *That Was Then, This Is Now*, in *New York Times Book Review*, August 8, 1971, p. 8.

Daly, Jay, *Presenting S. E. Hinton*, Twayne Publishers, 1987, pp. 41-43, 46-47.

Gilbert, Martin, *A History of the Twentieth Century*, Vol. 3, *1952–1999*, Perennial, 2000, p. 307.

Hinton, S. E., "S. E. Hinton," in *Speaking for Ourselves: Autobiographical Sketches by Notable Authors of Books for Young Adults*, edited by Donald R. Gallo, 1990, p. 95.

———, *That Was Then, This Is Now*, Laurel Leaf Books, 1985.

Lyons, Gene, "On Tulsa's Mean Streets," in *Newsweek*, Vol. 100, No. 15, October 11, 1982, pp. 105-06.

Malone, Michael, "Tough Puppies," in *Nation*, Vol. 242, No. 9, March 8, 1986, pp. 276-78, 290.

McMurtry, Larry, *The Last Picture Show*, Dial Press, 1966.

Olson, James S., and Randy Roberts, "Johnson's Escalation and the Antiwar Movement," in *The 1960s*, edited by William Dudley, Greenhaven Press, Inc., 2000, pp. 110-11, originally published in *Where the Domino Fell: America and Vietnam, 1945–1995*, St. Martin's Press, 1996.

Review of *That Was Then, This Is Now*, in *Times Literary Supplement*, No. 3634, October 22, 1971, p. 1318.

Roberts, J. M., *Twentieth Century: The History of the World, 1901 to 2000*, Penguin Books, 1999, p. 673.

Steigerwald, David, "The Antiwar Movement," in *The Sixties and the End of Modern America*, St. Martin's Press, 1995, originally published in *The 1960s*, edited by William Dudley, Greenhaven Press, Inc., 2000, pp. 138-39.

Further Reading

Baum, Dan, *Smoke and Mirrors: The War on Drugs and the Politics of Failure*, Little, Brown & Company, 1997.

> This retrospective look at the United States' war on drugs deviates from other books in this genre, which tend to use anecdotes to depict the government as deliberate participants in the spread of drugs. Instead, Baum, a journalist, provides balanced criticism about why the war on drugs has failed, using facts to back up his assertions.

Burkett, B. G., *Stolen Valor: How the Vietnam Generation Was Robbed of Its Heroes and Its History*, Verity Press, 1998.

> Burkett, a Vietnam veteran and reporter, was featured on the newsmagazine show *20/20* for this unflinching look at the ways in which Vietnam veterans have been misunderstood, in part due to the actions of some who have tarnished the image of this generation. Exhaustively researched, the book helps to set the record straight about a very painful time in American history.

Marshall, Joseph E., and Lonnie Wheeler, *Street Soldier: One Man's Struggle to Save a Generation, One Life at a Time*, VisionLines Publishing, 2000.

> About the time Hinton was writing *The Outsiders*, Marshall was starting his career teaching in a poor section of San Francisco, where young people often faced the issues Hinton wrote about. Two decades later, with the introduction of guns and drugs like crack into the schools, the situation worsened, and Marshall took action. This book details the inspiring story of how he started the Omega Boys Club and began to reach a group of troubled black teens from the ghetto, helping many of them get on track and go to college.

Miller, Timothy, *The Hippies and American Values*, University of Tennessee Press, 1991.

> Miller's information-packed book goes a long way towards setting the record straight about the main beliefs that hippies and the counterculture maintained and demonstrates the massive impact that hippies have had on American culture since the 1960s. The book features a bibliography of well-known and obscure underground newspapers, trivia facts, such as when the first Earth Day took place, and pictures of rock

groups and posters.

Printed in the USA
CPSIA information can be obtained
at www.ICGtesting.com
CBHW052205300624
10921CB00022B/370